National S...
Scheme Syllabus
& Logbook

© RYA National Sailing Scheme Syllabus & Logbook

Copyright RYA 2014

Third edition 2014
Reprinted May 2014
Reprinted February 2015

The Royal Yachting Association
RYA House, Ensign Way,
Hamble, Southampton,
Hampshire SO31 4YA

Tel: 0844 556 9555
Fax: 0844 556 9516
E-mail: publications@rya.org.uk
Web: www.rya.org.uk
Follow us on Twitter @RYAPublications or on YouTube

ISBN 978-1-906435998
RYA Order Code G4

All rights reserved. No part of this publication may be reproduced, stored in a retrieval system, or transmitted, in any form or by any means, electronic, mechanical, photocopying, recording or otherwise, without prior permission in writing from the publishers.

Sailing is a fantastic and diverse sport, with activities to suit everyone. The RYA National Sailing Scheme has been designed to help you enjoy whichever aspect of the sport that appeals to you. All the courses in the Scheme can be taken in a dinghy, keelboat or multihull so you can have tuition in whatever type of boat you wish.

Good sailing!

Amanda Van Santen
RYA Chief Instructor, Dinghy & Windsurfing

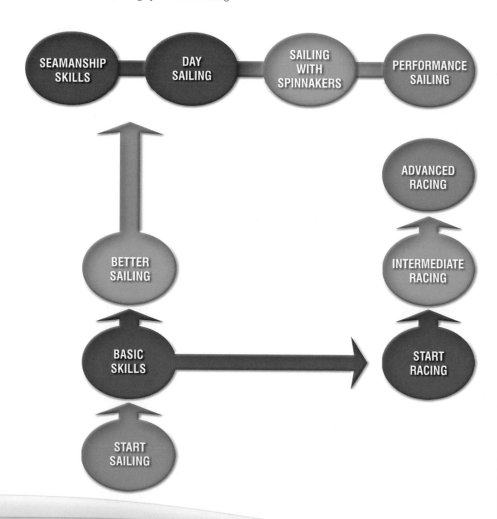

CONTENTS

How to find the right sailing course

The reputation of the RYA National Sailing Scheme has been built on high standards and good tuition. RYA Training Centres vary according to the sailing area available and the type of boats and level of tuition on offer. Whether you wish to learn to sail locally or improve your sailing on holiday, there should be an RYA Training Centre to suit you. To select a course that will meet your needs, visit the RYA website www.rya.org.uk/wheresmynearest for a list of sailing schools near you.

Some RYA Training Centres have specialised facilities (including boats) for people with disabilities. Others can offer integrated courses in standard boats. Some students with disabilities may need additional help to complete the full requirements for an RYA certificate. There is provision within the Scheme for certificates to be endorsed as appropriate. Please contact the Principal of your selected RYA Training Centre or the RYA for more information.

What is an RYA Recognised Training Centre?

Safety is a priority for the RYA. Each RYA Training Centre is regularly inspected for standards of tuition, facilities and equipment, as laid down by RYA Training and published in the guidance notes. All must have qualified staff, suitable boats and adequate safety cover. RYA Training Centres should display a Certificate of Recognition specifying the activities for which they are recognised. They are also required to carry public liability insurance.

For Beginners' courses run in single-handed dinghies, there should be an instructor to a maximum of 6 students in single-handed dinghies, or 1 to 3 in crewed dinghies with the instructor on board. Keelboat courses can be run with an instructor/student ratio of up to 1 to 4.

Training carried out in coastal conditions that are not tidal should include the tidal material in the relevant sections.

At the end of your course, the Principal or Chief Instructor will decide whether certificates are to be awarded. Certificates are specific to the type of boat used, i.e. dinghy, keelboat or multihull. If the Principal decides that further practice is necessary before awarding you a certificate, they will explain the reasons to you. Should you feel it necessary to appeal against the outcome, contact RYA Training for guidance.

The courses

All the courses in the RYA National Sailing Scheme can be completed in just two days, or spread over a series of sessions covering a period of 16 hours. Most are flexible and often available as evening or half-day sessions.

Direct assessments

Experienced sailors may wish to have direct assessment of their skills rather than taking part in a training course. The criteria are outlined in this book. Individual items will be signed off by the assessing instructor and the declaration signed by the Principal or Chief Instructor.

What next?

After taking your course you may consider joining a club, or buying a boat and joining the class association, who organise a variety of events. The RYA website (www.rya.org.uk) is a good place to find a club or locate your class association.

How to become an instructor

Having learnt to sail, you may enjoy passing your skills on to others. The RYA Instructor is an experienced sailor who has successfully completed a sailing test (the pre-entry test) and an instructor training course. Further information is on the RYA website.

RYA Instructors should also hold a first aid certificate and the RYA Powerboat Level 2 Certificate. Full details are contained in RYA publication G14, RYA National Sailing Scheme Instructor Handbook.

Courses for young people

The RYA also offers a training scheme for young people, the Youth Sailing Scheme. Full details are published in RYA book G11. Following completion of the Youth Sailing Scheme, young people may participate in further training through the advanced modules of the National Sailing Scheme.

Windsurfing, Powerboating, Sail and Power Cruising

The RYA organises similar training schemes for all these activities. Full details are available from the website or the RYA Training Department.

Learning resources

The RYA produces a wide range of materials to help you learn, from course handbooks to training DVDs. These can be obtained through RYA Training Centres and the RYA website.

> Are you aged between 14 to 24 and fancy challenging yourself?

The RYA is recognised as a National Operating Authority for The Duke of Edinburgh's Award (DofE). The DofE is a voluntary, non-competitive programme of activities for anyone aged 14 to 24, providing a fantastic opportunity to experience new activities or develop existing skills.

There are three progressive levels of programmes that, when successfully completed, lead to a Bronze, Silver or Gold Award.

Sailing as part of your DofE

Achieving a DofE Award can be made an adventure from beginning to end. Within an RYA club or training centre there are already many activities you could take part in that can count towards your DofE. These could range from:

Volunteering

Helping out at your local training centre, club or Team15 night on a regular basis. This could be as an assistant, in the kitchen or maybe even on the committee!

Physical

Regularly taking part in sailing or windsurfing activity? Why not set yourself a goal to gain a certain certificate in the RYA National Sailing or Windsurfing scheme, or maybe participate in regular club racing?

Skill

All about developing your skills, whether practical, social or personal. You may choose to sharpen up your powerboating, learn a new skill such as boat repair work, become an instructor or perhaps increase your theory knowledge and learn all about meteorology!

Residential and Expedition

You may never have been away from home before, let alone used your board or boat to go on an exciting adventure with friends, so now is the time!

Further information can be found, explaining the opportunities available, on the DofE website www.dofe.org, and the RYA website www.rya.org.uk/go/dofe.

START SAILING

This course provides a short introduction to sailing for novices. By the end of the course you will have the basic understanding of dinghy-handling techniques and background knowledge. It is recommended that all participants consolidate this short introduction with the Basic Skills and Better Sailing courses.

Duration: Approximately 16 hours (either spread over a series of sessions or 2 full days).

> Practical

Has a practical understanding of:

Rigging

Spars and rigging, parts of the sail, sail controls and foils

Has wind awareness ashore

Sailing techniques and manoeuvres

Wind awareness afloat

Reaching – sailing across the wind

Stopping – Lying-to

Controlling speed

Getting out of irons

Tacking – turning the front of the boat through the wind

Sailing upwind

The Five Essentials

Sailing downwind

Gybing – turning the back of the boat through the wind, from a training run

Importance of good communication when manoeuvring (double handers)

Can perform a basic capsize recovery, understands the importance of staying with the boat* (Optional)

Launching and recovery*

Can:

Secure a boat on the trolley

Understands the principles of:

Wheeling a trolley clear of other boats and overhead cables

Launching and leaving the shore

Coming ashore and recovery of a boat

Ropework

Can tie a figure of eight knot, round turn and two half hitches and secure a rope to a cleat

> Sailing Theory

Has theoretical understanding of:

Clothing and equipment

Knows the importance of personal safety, clothing and buoyancy

Sailing background

An awareness of other water users

Basic rules of the road – Avoid a collision at all costs, power/sail, port/starboard, overtaking boat, windward boat

Visual methods of attracting attention

Meteorology

Has an awareness of onshore and offshore winds

Sources of weather information and their relevance:

Effects on sailing location

Beaufort Scale

Conditions appropriate to ability and sailing location

> Keelboat Sailors

Clothing and equipment

Understands:

Use of, and correct fitting of lifejackets

Use of a safety harness if fitted

Man overboard recovery

Understands:

Actions to be taken to recover a man overboard

Man overboard recovery

Use of mooring lines

Emergency equipment and precautions

Has knowledge and awareness of:

Potential hazards of fuel and gas

Emergency equipment and precautions

Stowage and use of fire extinguishers

Other aspects

Basic Skills Course

> Chief Instructor's/Principal's Signature

> RYA Training Centre

*Not necessarily applicable to keelboats.

BASIC SKILLS

On completion of this course, you will have a basic knowledge of sailing and be capable of sailing without an instructor on board in light winds. It will be assumed that every student starting this course has already mastered the practical skills and absorbed the background knowledge required for Start Sailing. Both courses can be combined. Dinghy or multihull capsize recovery will be conducted in a controlled manner, one boat at a time, with a suitable rescue boat in attendance.

Duration: Approximately 16 hours (either spread over a series of sessions or 2 full days).

> Practical

Has a practical understanding of:

Rigging

How to rig according to weather conditions

Reefing ashore*

Sailing techniques and manoeuvres

Leaving and returning to a beach, jetty or mooring

Coming alongside a moored boat

Sailing in close company

Performing a man overboard recovery

Is aware of lee shore dangers

The Five Essentials

Can tack while sailing upwind, showing refined skill, losing minimal ground

Can gybe in a controlled manner while sailing downwind

Shows good communication when manoeuvring (Double-handers)

Understands and shows awareness of other water users

Can sail around a short course using all points of sail and crewing skills

Ropework

Can tie a bowline, clove hitch and reef knot

Capsize recovery

Can right a capsized boat using one method of righting and has knowledge of at least one other

Racing

Understands the course and starting procedure (May be covered as onshore teaching)

> Keelboat Sailors

Rigging

Can reef afloat

Ropework

Can use winches

Use of engines (if fitted)

Has knowledge of engine checks, starting, stopping and running procedures

Can come alongside and pick up a mooring

Sailing techniques and manoeuvres

Can:

Anchor

Sail using transits

Emergency equipment and precautions

Knows the importance of first aid kits and flares including stowage

> Multihull Sailors

Sailing techniques and manoeuvres

Understands the basic principles of crew weight, airflow, technique (CAT)

> Sailing Theory

Has theoretical understanding of:

Clothing and equipment

Knows the importance of personal safety, clothing, basic personal and boat buoyancy

Launching and recovery

Boat storage ashore, launching and recovery

Sailing background

Has knowledge of:

Basic rules of the road; avoid collisions at all costs, power/sail, port/starboard, windward boat, overtaking boat

Basic advice for independent sailing:

Self-reliance and basic equipment

Visual methods of attracting attention

Has knowledge of:

The points of sailing and the 'No go Zone'

How a sail works

How a sailing boat moves (basic theory)

Meteorology

Has knowledge of:

Sources of relevant weather, inshore forecasts and their interpretation

The Beaufort Wind Scale

Understands when to reef

Has knowledge of a simple synoptic chart

> Coastal Waters

Can apply the practical section in coastal waters

Understands:

How to apply weather forecasts in coastal waters

Tide tables, tidal sequence of springs and neaps, ebb and flow

Speed over ground with/against tidal flow

The effect of wind direction and tidal flow on sailing conditions

The importance of informing someone ashore and the dangers of sailing alone

Knows how to access local information and advice for sea sailing

Other aspects

Better Sailing Course

Opportunities for regular activity (local club and centre activity and groups, etc.)

Purchasing your own equipment

Basic racing

> Chief Instructor's/Principal's Signature

> RYA Training Centre

*Not necessarily applicable to keelboats.

On completion of the course the successful sailor will be safety conscious and capable of sailing without an instructor on board in light to moderate conditions. This improver course seeks to bridge the gap between Start Sailing, Basic Skills and the five Advanced modules by offering an introduction to the different modules, allowing sailors to select better their preferred route within the sport. Better Sailing is intended to make the transition easier for those sailors wishing to progress further through the scheme, allowing for opportunity to practise and consolidate sailing techniques and experience some of the activities the Advanced modules have to offer, helping to build confidence and support development of good technique and independent sailing. Additional module options are non-compulsory for completion of the Better Sailing course. They are designed to provide an introduction to the various aspects of sailing. Which elements are chosen should be discussed by student and instructor. Where practicable, students should be provided with the opportunity to sail different dinghies during the course, single and double-handers.

Duration: Approximately 16 hours (either spread over a series of sessions or 2 full days).

> Practical

Has a practical understanding of:

Sailing techniques and manoeuvres

Understands how to use rig and sail controls to prepare the boat according to different weather conditions and sea states

Can check a spinnaker is rigged correctly (if fitted)

Core skills

Can:

Leave and return to a shore, jetty or mooring (including windward and leeward shore in light conditions)

Recover a man overboard effectively

Use the sail telltales effectively

Reef a sail when required

Demonstrate a 'dry capsize'

Understands how to avoid inversion

Sail using efficient and skilful application of the Five Essentials

Tack – maintaining boat speed and balance, upwind

Gybe – maintaining boat speed and balance

Show good use of crew and to best effect (where applicable)

Understands when, and the importance of manoeuvre timing

> Sailing Background

Has theoretical understanding of:

The IRPCS, and can apply them to:

Other sailing vessels

Power-driven vessels

Following or crossing narrow channels

Action by stand-on vessel

Has basic sail-control knowledge to change the sail shape and power

Understands:

The points of sailing

The Five Essentials

Basic meteorology terminology, including the Beaufort Scale

Can obtain a weather forecast

Can interpret a basic synoptic chart

Has awareness of changing weather conditions

> Additional Module Options:

Has both practical and theoretical understanding of the following:

Seamanship skills

Can demonstrate anchoring in various conditions

Introduction to sailing in adverse conditions (centreboardless, rudderless sailing)

Race skills

Has knowledge of the 'simplified ISAF Racing Rules of Sailing'

Can:

Start and finish a simple race

Choose the best route to sail around a course, depending on conditions (using the Five Essentials)

Day sailing skills

Basic chart orientation – including cardinal and lateral buoyage systems

Take bearings and measure distances on a chart

The effect of tide and wind direction on sailing conditions

Can:

Use a local tide table

Follow a pre-planned route

Spinnaker sailing skills

Basic introduction to spinnaker handling as crew or helm, including rig, hoist and drop

Performance sailing skills

Basic introduction to trapezing with instructor on the helm (Optional – boat-dependant)

Introduction to better hiking technique

Other aspects

The Advanced modules

Opportunities to sail regularly

Introduction to high-performance boats

Local club racing

> Chief Instructor's/Principal's Signature

> RYA Training Centre

On successful completion of this course, you will be capable of manoeuvring a dinghy/keelboat/multihull in a seamanlike manner and making seamanship decisions in moderate conditions.

It will be assumed that when starting on this course you have already mastered the practical skills and absorbed the background knowledge required for the previous levels.

Tuition will be given by trained instructors, using appropriate supervision ratios with regard to the location and competence of the students. Much of the work afloat will be done without an instructor aboard. The emphasis is on increasing the self-reliance and decision-making of the sailor.

Duration: Approximately 16 hours (either spread over a series of sessions or 2 full days).

> Practical

Ropework

Can tie a fisherman's bend, rolling hitch and sheet bend

Can demonstrate heat sealing and whipping

Launching and recovery

Can leave and return to beach, jetty or mooring, including windward and leeward shore

Sailing techniques and manoeuvres

Can:

Heave to

Reef afloat

Recover man overboard

Be towed by a power vessel

Anchor, including principles and techniques for different circumstances†

Sail backwards

Sail in adverse circumstances (no rudder, no centreboard)*†

Knows how to prepare road trailer and secure a boat for transportation (optional)

> Sailing Background

Sailing theory and background

Understands the following terminology:

Windward, leeward, abeam, forward, aft, ahead, astern, to weather, downwind, amidships, quarter, pinching, sailing by the lee, luff, bear away, planing, sternway, broaching

Knows and can apply the following International Regulations for the Prevention of Collisions at Sea (IRPCS):

Meeting other sailing vessels, meeting power-driven vessels, following or crossing narrow channels, action by stand-on vessel

Capsize Recovery

Knows how to recover from total inversion (practical session if possible)

Meteorology

Knows sources of information on weather patterns for the day

Can interpret forecasts and understand local effects

Aware of Beaufort Wind Scale and changing weather conditions, including fog

> Coastal (Optional)

Capable of practical application of Section A on coastal waters

Can use local tide tables

Understands rate of rise and fall – Twelfths Rule

Is aware of tidal streams

Has a basic understanding of charts and important symbols

> Experienced Sailor's Direct Assesment

The candidate must present logged evidence of at least two seasons' sailing experience. The candidate will satisfactorily complete all of Section A and shall, afloat and ashore, satisfactorily answer questions on Section B. Candidates seeking assessment on coastal waters will demonstrate knowledge of Section C.

> Chief Instructor's/Principal's Signature

> RYA Training Centre

*Not necessarily applicable to keelboats.
†Not necessarily applicable to multihulls.

On successful completion of this course, you will have a confident, safe approach to planning and executing a short day sail in a dinghy/keelboat/multihull.

On starting this course you should have already mastered the practical skills and absorbed the background knowledge required for the previous levels. In addition, sailors wishing to cruise independently should ensure that they understand and can carry out the manoeuvres in the Seamanship Skills (see page 14) part of the RYA National Sailing Scheme.

Tuition will be given by trained instructors, supervised by a Coastal Senior Instructor, using appropriate supervision ratios with regard to the location and competence of the students. The course will include the planning and execution of a day sail.

Students will be kept informed of their individual progress throughout the course.

Candidates who hold the RYA Basic Navigation Completion Certificate or a higher-level RYA cruising award may gain exemption from the chartwork part of Section B.

Duration: Approximately 16 hours (either spread over a series of sessions or 2 full days).

> Practical

Rigging

Can prepare and equip a boat for cruising including safety and navigation equipment, clothing and food, and stow gear correctly

Sailing techniques and manoeuvres

Can plan and undertake a day sail including a consideration of pilotage/navigation and collision avoidance

Can use anchor to effect lee shore landing and departure*†

Adverse conditions

Is able to self-rescue following total inversion*

Understands how to improvise in the event of gear failure

> Sailing Background

Sailing theory and background

Has knowledge of boat handling in strong winds and difficult conditions (practical where possible)

Navigation

Can plan a day's cruise in coastal waters, including knowledge of:

Publications available, particularly charts, tide tables, tidal stream atlases

Navigational instruments and their limitations afloat

Use of GPS including waypoint navigation

Confirming position by another source

Tidal heights and tidal streams (Rule of Twelfths or percentage rule), probable changes in the weather and the interaction of weather and tidal streams

Decision-making in adverse circumstances including planning alternatives and refuges

Magnetic compass: Variation and Deviation

Interpretation of charts

Use of transits and bearings to steer course and fix position

Recording position and principles of dead reckoning

Meteorology

Knows sources of information on weather patterns for the day. Understands main characteristics of high- and low-pressure systems and simple interpretation of synoptic charts

Has awareness of changing weather conditions

> Experienced Sailor's Direct Assessment

The candidate must present logged evidence of at least two seasons' sailing experience. The candidate will complete all of Section A, demonstrating a competent, purposeful and safe approach. He will answer questions on Section B and wherever possible demonstrate skills satisfactorily afloat and ashore.

> Chief Instructor's/Principal's Signature

> RYA Training Centre

*Not necessarily applicable to keelboats.
†Not necessarily applicable to multihulls.

On successful completion of this course you will understand how to sail a dinghy/keelboat/ multihull rigged with an asymmetric or symmetric spinnaker. It is assumed when starting this course you have already mastered the practical skills and absorbed the background knowledge required for previous levels. Tuition will be given by an Advanced Instructor, or by an Instructor with appropriate experience approved by the Principal, using appropriate supervision ratios with regard to the location and competence of the students.

Duration: Approximately 16 hours (either spread over a series of sessions or 2 full days).

> Practical

Rigging

Can rig boats including spinnaker, and trapeze where fitted

Launching and recovery

Understands how to launch boats with open transoms and/or racks*†

Sailing techniques and manoeuvres

Can sail as crew or helm using equipment to good advantage

Can perform spinnaker hoist, gybe and drop as crew or helm

Understands and can sail best course downwind

Capsize recovery

Can perform capsize recovery including spinnaker

Knows how to recover from total inversion*

> Sailing Background

Racing

Has knowledge of courses for type of boat

Sailing theory and background

Understands the concept of apparent wind sailing

Understands the effect of hull shape on performance

Can access sources of information and apply rig set-up for different conditions

> Experienced Sailor's Direct Assessment

Candidates will complete all of Section A, demonstrating a competent, purposeful and confident approach to an Advanced Instructor, satisfactorily answering questions on Section B afloat and ashore.

> Chief Instructor's/Principal's Signature

> RYA Training Centre

*Not necessarily applicable to keelboats.
†Not necessarily applicable to multihulls.

On successful completion of this course, you will understand how to sail performance dinghies/keelboats/multihulls in all wind conditions that you can expect to encounter, sailing the boat to best advantage at all times. The emphasis is on coaching to improve your sailing performance and therefore will involve coaching from powerboats. This course is intended primarily for two-person spinnaker boats; however, it may be delivered in performance single-handers and the certificate endorsed accordingly.

Tuition will be given by an Advanced Instructor for the type of boat, using appropriate supervision ratios with regard to the location and competence of the students and the need to provide continuous feedback on the water. It is assumed that every student starting this course has already mastered the practical skills and absorbed the background knowledge required for previous levels. In practical terms, at least a full season's sailing experience since learning to sail is advisable.

Duration: Approximately 16 hours (either spread over a series of sessions or 2 full days).

> Practical

Rigging

Can rig any type of boat, including spinnaker and trapeze (if fitted)

Understands basic rig setup and tuning

Sailing techniques and manoeuvres

Can make best possible use of crew and equipment to sail efficiently on all points of sailing in a variety of conditions, including symmetric or asymmetric spinnaker

Can use sail controls to effect changes to shape and power of sails

Can spot and use windshifts and gusts to effect best course up and down wind

Can perform capsize recovery including spinnaker. Knows how to recover from total inversion*

Can tack, refining skills according to conditions

Shows understanding of roll tacking principles

Can gybe, refining skills according to conditions

Shows understanding of roll gybing principles

> Sailing Background

Sailing theory and background

Understands how to make use of wind variation and tidal eddies which occur due to geographical features and tidal conditions

Has an understanding of hull shapes and rig types, including their effect on performance

Understands planing and the effect of rails

Meteorology

Knows sources of information on weather patterns for the day

Understands main characteristics of high- and low-pressure systems and simple interpretation of synoptic charts

Has awareness of changing weather conditions

Experienced Sailor's Direct Assessment

The candidate must present logged evidence of at least two seasons' sailing experience. The candidate will complete all of Section A, demonstrating a competent, purposeful and safe approach to sailing performance boats. The candidate will answer questions on Section B afloat and ashore.

> Chief Instructor's/Principal's Signature

> RYA Training Centre

*Not necessarily applicable to keelboats.

This course is designed to give the confidence, skills and knowledge to take part in club racing in good conditions. Confidence is essential if the sailor is to enjoy racing. The course involves the sailor in a range of enjoyable exercises designed to build confidence and to improve skills through practice. It is assumed that every student starting this course has already mastered the practical skills and absorbed the background knowledge required for previous levels.

Physical and mental preparation

Has knowledge of:

Food as fuel

Keeping hydrated

Boat preparation

Has knowledge of:

Availability of class tuning guides

Basic tuning

Boat handling

Has a basic understanding of:

Making best use of the Five
Essentials as Helm

Crew (Double-handers only)

Mark rounding

Laylines

Hiking

Boat speed

Understands how to alter sail controls
both round the course and for differing
conditions

Teamwork (for double-handers)

Understands the requirements to develop
a good partnership

Strategy and meteorology

Can obtain and understand a simple
weather forecast

Has knowledge of clean air, gusts
and lulls

Racing rules

Has a basic understanding of the Racing
Rules of Sailing (part 2, section a)

**Has an understanding of the basic rights
of way rules:**

Port/starboard (rule 10)

Windward boat (rule 11)

Clear ahead/clear astern (rule 12)

Tacking (rule 13)

Tactics

Has knowledge of basic boat-on-boat
situations

Starts

Has knowledge of transits

Can demonstrate the basics
of starting

Other aspects

An introduction to local club racing

> Chief Instructor's/Principal's Signature

> RYA Training Centre

This course builds on the knowledge and skills learnt from 'Start Racing', developing greater awareness of the key principles of starting, boat handling, boat speed, strategy and tactics, through course time and regular race activity.

Physical and mental preparation

Understands the importance of fitness
for sailing ▢

Boat preparation

Has knowledge of:

How to use a tuning guide ▢
How to set a boat up for
specific conditions ▢

Understands:

How to prepare a boat for club racing, including:

Hull ▢
Spars ▢
Sails ▢
Foils ▢
Fittings ▢
Rigging ▢
Control lines ▢

Boat handling

Has knowledge of how to steer the boat
without the rudder ▢

Understands the principles involved in:

Slow-speed handling, including:
Stopping ▢
Accelerating ▢
Sailing backwards ▢
Roll tacking ▢
Roll gybing ▢

Boat speed

Has knowledge of basic aerodynamics:

How a sail works ▢
How to power up the rig ▢
How to de-power the rig ▢
Weather helm ▢
Lee helm ▢
Understands how to set up the boat for a
range of conditions ▢

Teamwork (double-handers)

Understands how to divide up the:

Roles around the course ▢
Jobs in the boat ▢

Strategy and meteorology

Understands:

Clean air ▢
Gusts ▢
Lulls ▢
How to interpret a weather forecast in
relation to the sailing venue ▢

Racing rules

Understands:

Has a good understanding of Part 1/Section A
and the Definitions of the Racing Rules ▢
Basic understanding of Sections B/C/D ▢
Understands how to sail by the
Racing Rules ▢

Tactics

Understands:

Boat-on-boat tactics ▢
Lee bow situation ▢
How to cover and break cover ▢
Importance of clean air ▢

Starts

Understands bias, and how to assess it ▢

Has knowledge of:

How to hold boat on line (hovering) ▢
Accelerating off the line ▢

Other aspects

Has knowledge of and participates regularly
in club and open meetings ▢

> Chief Instructor's/Principal's Signature

> RYA Training Centre

A predominately practical course, Advanced Racing is all about developing skills in preparation for open meetings and higher-level competition.

Mental and physical preparation

Understands how to, and the value of, goal setting

Boat preparation

Understands how to:

Improve foil finish

Optimise boat to class rules

Use a tuning guide

Boat handling

Understands the principles of:

Steering with sails

Balance

Can demonstrate these principles in taking penalty turns

Can demonstrate good techniques in a full range of conditions:

Tacking

Gybing

Boat speed

Understands:

Relevance of sail controls and effects on the sail(s)

How to change gears in different conditions while on the water

How to vary the tuning guide for different conditions

How to create your own tuning guide

How to create your own post-race analysis sheet

Teamwork (double-handers)

Understands effective:

Race analysis

Race and training goals

Can:

Communicate effectively

React to changing circumstances

Strategy and meteorology

Can create a race strategy prior to going afloat based on weather forecasts and tide tables etc.

Racing rules

Has good knowledge and understanding of the Racing Rules of Sailing, Part 2

Understands the RYA Racing Charter

Tactics

Has knowledge of:

Holding a lane upwind

Boat-on-fleet tactics

Attacking

Controlling situations

Understands:

Boat-on-group tactics

Overtaking and defending tactics

Covering

Different approaches to marks – when to gybe or bear away

Starts

Understands pre-start rules

Can:

Protect a gap to leeward

Hold the boat on the line (hovering)

Use transits

Has knowledge of:

Various start sequences

Recall signals

Starting penalties

Other aspects

Participates regularly in:

Open meetings

National class events

> Chief Instructor's/Principal's Signature

> RYA Training Centre

If you have enjoyed your experiences of learning to sail and developing your sailing techniques and skills through the RYA National Sailing Scheme, why not consider sharing your enthusiasm, expertise and skills with others by becoming involved in the RYA instructor training programme? Below are brief details concerning the basic training courses. More information can be found in G14 RYA National Sailing Scheme Instructor Handbook.

RYA Assistant Instructor

Duration: 2 days / 20 hours

The RYA Assistant Instructor is trained to assist qualified instructors to teach beginners up to the standard of the RYA National Sailing Scheme Level 2 and the RYA Youth Sailing Scheme Stage 3. They must only work under the supervision of a Senior Instructor. The award is centre-specific.

Eligibility for the training course

Pass one of the RYA National Sailing Scheme Advanced Modules or equivalent personal sailing standard.

Recommendation by Principal of training centre.

Training

Training will cover the centre's safe-operation procedures and the teaching points related to teaching beginners. The award is centre-specific. Training is based on a two-day or modular course of 20 hours' duration at the centre run by the Principal/Chief Instructor who holds a valid RYA Senior Instructor certificate.

Assessment

Candidates will be assessed on their practical teaching ability with beginners. Successful candidates will be awarded an RYA Assistant Instructor certificate by their Principal.

Dinghy/Keelboat/Multihull Instructor

Duration: 5 days / 50 hours

It is possible to complete the RYA National Sailing Scheme in dinghies, keelboats or multihulls. Therefore, instructors teaching the scheme must be qualified for the type of boat in which they will be teaching. The instructor certificate will show whether the instructor is qualified to teach on inland or coastal waters (depending on where they completed the pre-entry sailing assessment and course).

Role

- Competent, experienced sailor able to sail in strong winds
- Can teach RYA National Sailing Scheme up to and including Seamanship Skills, Day Sailing, Sailing with Spinnakers and RYA Youth Sailing Scheme Stages 1–4
- Will only work under the supervision of the RYA Senior Instructor

Eligibility for the training course

- Minimum age 16
- Valid first aid certificate (see www.rya.org.uk/go/firstaidcertificates)
- RYA Powerboat Level 2 certificate
- Pre-entry sailing assessment completed
- RYA membership

Training

- The structure and content of the RYA National Sailing Scheme and RYA Youth Sailing Scheme
- Training in RYA teaching methods including teaching both adults and children
- Preparation and presentation of a lesson
- Preparation and use of visual aids
- The assessment of students' abilities
- The use of powered craft in a teaching environment

Assessment

- The assessment will be based on an overall (or holistic) judgement throughout the week and during the instructor moderation day.

This assessment will include:

- Enthusiasm for the sport
- Sailing ability
- Confidence and knowledge in the subject
- Awareness of safety
- Practical teaching according to RYA methods
- Theory knowledge
- Successful demonstrations and clear explanations
- Correct diagnosis and tactful correction of students' faults
- Safe powerboat handling in a teaching environment

PERSONAL LOG

DATE	TYPE OF BOAT	HOURS' EXPERIENCE		ACTIVITY & WEATHER CONDITIONS		AUTHORISATION
		HELM	CREW	TYPE OF COURSE OR ACTIVITY	MAX WIND SPEED	CENTRE/CLUB INSTRUCTOR

DATE	TYPE OF BOAT	HOURS' EXPERIENCE		ACTIVITY & WEATHER CONDITIONS		AUTHORISATION
		HELM	CREW	TYPE OF COURSE OR ACTIVITY	MAX WIND SPEED	CENTRE/CLUB INSTRUCTOR

**PLEASE ATTACH YOUR
RYA CERTIFICATE HERE**

Please note that no record of
certificates is held by the RYA

Enquiries about lost certificates
should be made to the centre
where the course was taken

**PLEASE ATTACH YOUR
RYA CERTIFICATE HERE**

Please note that no record of
certificates is held by the RYA

Enquiries about lost certificates
should be made to the centre
where the course was taken

**PLEASE ATTACH YOUR
RYA CERTIFICATE HERE**

Please note that no record of
certificates is held by the RYA

Enquiries about lost certificates
should be made to the centre
where the course was taken

**PLEASE ATTACH YOUR
RYA CERTIFICATE HERE**

Please note that no record of
certificates is held by the RYA

Enquiries about lost certificates
should be made to the centre
where the course was taken

**PLEASE ATTACH YOUR
RYA CERTIFICATE HERE**

Please note that no record of
certificates is held by the RYA

Enquiries about lost certificates
should be made to the centre
where the course was taken

**PLEASE ATTACH YOUR
RYA CERTIFICATE HERE**

Please note that no record of
certificates is held by the RYA

Enquiries about lost certificates
should be made to the centre
where the course was taken

**PLEASE ATTACH YOUR
RYA CERTIFICATE HERE**

Please note that no record of
certificates is held by the RYA

Enquiries about lost certificates
should be made to the centre
where the course was taken

**PLEASE ATTACH YOUR
RYA CERTIFICATE HERE**

Please note that no record of
certificates is held by the RYA

Enquiries about lost certificates
should be made to the centre
where the course was taken

**PLEASE ATTACH YOUR
RYA CERTIFICATE HERE**

Please note that no record of
certificates is held by the RYA

Enquiries about lost certificates
should be made to the centre
where the course was taken

**PLEASE ATTACH YOUR
RYA CERTIFICATE HERE**

Please note that no record of
certificates is held by the RYA

Enquiries about lost certificates
should be made to the centre
where the course was taken

Shop online at
www.rya.org.uk/shop

- Secure online ordering
- 15% discount for RYA members
- Books, DVDs, navigation aids and lots more
- Free delivery to a UK address for RYA members on orders over £25
- Free delivery to an overseas address for RYA members on orders over £50
- Buying online from the RYA shop enables the RYA in its work on behalf of its members